USING MATHS

CLIMB EVEREST

by Hilary Koll, Steve Mills
and Russell Brice

USING
MATHS
CLIMB EVEREST

Copyright © ticktock Entertainment Ltd 2006

First published in Great Britain in 2006 by ticktock Media Ltd.,
Unit 2, Orchard Business Centre, North Farm Road, Tunbridge Wells, Kent, TN2 3XF

ISBN 1 86007 987 3
Printed in China

510 KOL

HILARY KOLL
Hilary Koll (B.Ed. Hons) was a Leading Maths Teacher in a primary school before training as a Numeracy Consultant for the National Numeracy Strategy. She has worked as a Lecturer in Mathematics Education at the University of Reading, teaching on undergraduate, post-graduate and training courses. She is now a full-time writer and consultant in mathematics education. Hilary Koll and Steve Mills can be contacted via their website www.cmeprojects.com

STEVE MILLS
Steve Mills (B.A. Hons, P.G.C.E., M.Ed.) was a teacher of both primary and secondary age children and an LEA Maths Advisory Support Teacher before joining the University of Reading as a Lecturer in Mathematics Education. He worked with both under-graduate and post-graduate students in their preparation for teaching maths in schools. He has written many mathematics books for both teachers and children. Visit www.cmeprojects.com for details.

RUSSELL BRICE
Russell Brice has over 30 years experience in mountaineering. In 1988 he was the first climber to cross the infamous Pinnacles of the North East ridge of Everest. Russell runs Himalayan Experience Ltd a company that organises expeditions to mountains over 8000 metres. He is widely reputed as one of the most professional leaders of all guided expeditions to the Himalayas. Russell has climbed Everest 14 times, and has reached the summit twice.

CONTENTS

NUMERACY WORK COVERED IN THIS BOOK:

CALCULATIONS:
Throughout this book there are opportunities to practise **addition**, **subtraction**, **multiplication** and **division** using both mental calculation strategies and pencil and paper methods.

NUMBERS AND THE NUMBER SYSTEM:
- AVERAGES: pg. 23
- COMPARING AND ORDERING NUMBERS: pg. 6
- ESTIMATING: pgs. 6, 14, 15, 23, 27
- FRACTIONS: pgs. 20, 21, 26, 27
- NEGATIVE NUMBERS: pgs. 18, 19
- NUMBER PATTERNS: pgs. 8, 9
- NUMBER SEQUENCES: pgs. 8, 9
- PERCENTAGES: pgs. 14, 15, 26, 27
- VERY LARGE NUMBERS: pgs. 16, 17, 21

SOLVING 'REAL LIFE' PROBLEMS:
- DATE: pgs. 8, 9, 10, 11
- MONEY: pgs. 16, 17
- TEMPERATURE: pgs. 18, 19
- TIME: pgs. 8, 9, 11, 23, 24, 25
- WEIGHT: pgs. 12, 13, 16, 17

HANDLING DATA:
- TIMELINE: pgs. 10, 11
- READING A GRAPH: pgs. 14, 15, 19

MEASURES:
- CONVERTING METRIC/IMPERIAL MEASUREMENTS: pgs. 6, 7

SHAPE AND SPACE:
- 2-D SHAPES: pg. 26
- ANGLES: pg. 22
- COMPASS DIRECTIONS: pg. 22

Supports the maths work taught at Key Stage 2 and 3

HOW TO USE THIS BOOK

Maths is important in the lives of people everywhere. We use maths when we play a game, ride a bike, go shopping – in fact, all the time! Everyone needs to use maths at work. You may not realise it, but a climber would use maths during an expedition to the top of Mount Everest, the world's highest mountain. With this book you will get the chance to try lots of exciting maths activities using real life mountaineering data and facts about Everest. Practise your maths and numeracy skills and experience the thrill of what it's really like to climb to the top of the world.

This exciting maths book is very easy to use – check out what's inside!

Fun to read information about leading an expedition up Mount Everest.

MATHS ACTIVITIES

Look for the
EVEREST FILE.
You will find real life maths activities and questions to try.

To answer some of the questions, you will need to collect data from a DATA BOX. Sometimes, you will need to collect facts and data from the text or from charts and diagrams.

Be prepared! You will need a pen or pencil and a notebook for your workings and answers.

FITNESS PROGRAMME

To climb to the **summit** of Everest you need to be very fit and must start training months in advance. You need to plan ahead. Start a programme to improve your **cardiovascular** fitness (that's exercise that gets your heart pumping). Running, cycling and swimming are all good for cardiovascular fitness. Get climbing mountains in your own country. Do some weight lifting to improve your upper body strength, which you'll need for carrying your heavy rucksack and for digging out snow holes. It's also advisable to put on some extra weight as some people who try to climb Everest use up their body's fat reserves and run out of energy.

EVEREST FILE

In the DATA BOX on page 9 you will see information about a running schedule or plan.

1) If a person followed this plan for the whole of July:
   a) how many days off would they get?
   b) how many times would they run 8 miles?
   c) how far would they run in total?
2) If it takes about 7 minutes to run each mile, about how long will it take to run 8 miles?
3) Look at the dates of the days off in July. Identify the pattern.

(You will find a TIP to help you with these questions on page 28)

MENTAL ATTITUDE FACTS

In general the fitter you are, the more you enjoy climbing, because it takes less out of you. But just being fit doesn't mean you will cope with the altitude. A person who is not used to the lack of **oxygen** in the air is more likely to get altitude sickness. During an expedition there are long periods of time sitting around doing nothing while people acclimatise to new altitudes. Some people find this so frustrating that they leave the expedition without attempting to reach the summit at all. Climbing at altitude is hard. Even very fit people sometimes can't deal with the discomfort and pain involved and so don't make it to the summit, whereas others who are less fit succeed through sheer determination. Strong willpower and a real determination not to give up can be much more important than fitness.

8

Fun to read mountain facts.

DATA BOX

If you see one of these boxes, there will be important data inside that will help you with the maths activities.

MATHS ACTIVITIES

Feeling confident? Try these extra **CHALLENGE QUESTIONS.**

DATA BOX TRAINING PLAN

A person decides on a running training programme for one month, running over hills or on a treadmill carrying a rucksack. The distances run each day are shown on the calendar.

JULY						
Monday	Tuesday	Wednesday	Thursday	Friday	Saturday	Sunday
			1 8 miles	2 8 miles	3 8 miles	4 8 miles	🏃 DAY OFF
6 8 miles	7 8 miles	8 8 miles	9 8 miles	🏃 10 DAY OFF	11 8 miles	12 8 miles
13 8 miles	14 8 miles	🏃 15 DAY OFF	16 8 miles	17 8 miles	18 8 miles	19 8 miles
🏃 20 DAY OFF	21 8 miles	22 8 miles	23 8 miles	24 8 miles	🏃 25 DAY OFF	26 8 miles
27 8 miles	28 8 miles	29 8 miles	🏃 30 DAY OFF	31 8 miles		

CHALLENGE QUESTIONS

In the DATA BOX on this page you will see information about a running schedule or plan.

1) If a person followed this plan for the whole of July:
   a) how many times would they run on a Friday?
   b) how many times would they run on a Saturday?
   c) on which day of the week would they not get a day off?

2) If it takes about 7 minutes to run each mile, about how long will a person spend running in July if they followed this plan? Give your answer in hours and minutes.

3) A person began a training programme on 1 July. How many miles would be run in July if the pattern was:
   a) run 8 miles a day for 3 days, followed by 2 days off?
   b) run 8 miles a day for 2 days, followed by 1 day off?
   c) run 8 miles every other day?

(You will find a TIP to help you with these questions on page 28)

Climbing other high mountains will help you decide if you are ready to tackle Everest.

IF YOU NEED HELP...

TIPS FOR MATHS SUCCESS

On pages 28 – 29 you will find lots of tips to help you with your maths work.

ANSWERS

Turn to pages 30 – 31 to check your answers.
(Try all the activities and questions before you take a look at the answers.)

GLOSSARY

On page 32 there is a glossary of mountaineering words and a glossary of maths words. The glossary words appear **in bold** in the text.

9

KNOW YOUR MOUNTAIN

A group of people from all around the world is on an expedition to try to climb Mount Everest, the highest mountain on Earth. You have lots of experience in climbing high mountains, and so you have been invited to join the group! You don't know very much about Everest yet so you decide to find out about it. Did you know that Mount Everest has several different names? You must get to know where in the world it is, how far it is from where you live, how high it is and so on. Each of the people in the expedition group receives a map showing where Everest is and how far it is from different cities in the world.

EVEREST FILE

In the DATA BOX on page 7 you will see information about some of the highest mountains in the world.

Use the information to answer these questions.
Give your answers in metres.

1) How high is Everest?

2) Which is the fourth highest mountain in the world?

3) How much higher is Everest than
   a) Kanchenjunga?   e) K2?
   b) Dhaulagiri?   f) Lhotse?
   c) Makalu?   g) Cho Oyu?
   d) Manaslu?

4) 1 mile = 5280 feet
   Approximately how many miles is the height of Manaslu?

(You will find a TIP to help you with these questions on page 28)

MOUNTAIN FACTS

Mount Everest's height was first calculated as 8839.81 m, which was accepted as the correct height until 1955 when more sophisticated methods of measuring were used. Everest is now known to be exactly 8844.43 metres to the very top of the rock with about 3.5 m of snow on top. Before Everest was proved to be the highest mountain in the world, it was thought that Kanchenjunga was.

OTHER NAMES

• The Tibetan name for Everest is Qomolongma (pronounced 'Cho-mo-lung-ma'). It means Mother Goddess of the World.

• The name in Nepal is Sagarmatha (pronounced 'Sagar-math-a'). It means Forehead of the Ocean or Goddess of the Sky.

 **DATA BOX**

THE WORLD'S HIGHEST MOUNTAINS

These are the 8 highest mountains in the world.
All of the mountains are in the Himalaya mountain range.

Mountain	Other names	Height in metres	Height in feet	Country
Mount Everest	Qomolongma, Sagarmatha, Zhumulangma Feng	8844	29035	Nepal / China (Tibet)
Kanchenjunga		8586	28169	Nepal / India
Dhaulagiri		8167	26794	Nepal
Makalu		8462	27765	Nepal / China (Tibet)
Manaslu		8156	26758	Nepal
K2	Qogir, Godwin Austen	8611	28250	Pakistan
Lhotse		8516	27940	Nepal
Cho Oyu		8201	26906	Nepal / China (Tibet)

London 4600 miles

New York 7600 miles

Tokyo 3300 miles

Everest

Sydney 6100 miles

The distances on the map show approximately how far each city is from Everest.

Buenos Aires 10300 miles

Cape Town 6200 miles

Climbing Mount Everest is the ultimate ambition for many climbers.

CHALLENGE QUESTION

The map on this page shows where Everest is and some approximate distances from Everest to different parts of the world.

The distances are given in miles. To find the distance in kilometres, divide the number of miles by 5 and then multiply by 8. How far is it in kilometres from Everest to:

a) London   b) New York   c) Buenos Aires
d) Tokyo   e) Cape Town   f) Sydney

(You will find a TIP to help you with this question on page 28)

FITNESS PROGRAMME

To climb to the **summit** of Everest you need to be very fit and must start training months in advance. You need to plan ahead. Start a programme to improve your **cardiovascular** fitness (that's exercise that gets your heart pumping). Running, cycling and swimming are all good for cardiovascular fitness. Get climbing mountains in your own country. Do some weight lifting to improve your upper body strength, which you'll need for carrying your heavy rucksack and for digging out snow holes. It's also advisable to put on some extra weight as some people who try to climb Everest use up their body's fat reserves and run out of energy.

EVEREST FILE

In the DATA BOX on page 9 you will see information about a running schedule or plan.

1) If a person followed this plan for the whole of July:
   a) how many days off would they get?
   b) how many times would they run 8 miles?
   c) how far would they run in total?
2) If it takes about 7 minutes to run each mile, about how long will it take to run 8 miles?
3) Look at the dates of the days off in July. Identify the pattern.

(You will find a TIP to help you with these questions on page 28)

MENTAL ATTITUDE FACTS

In general the fitter you are, the more you enjoy climbing, because it takes less out of you. But just being fit doesn't mean you will cope with the altitude. A person who is not used to the lack of **oxygen** in the air is more likely to get altitude sickness. During an expedition there are long periods of time sitting around doing nothing while people acclimatise to new altitudes. Some people find this so frustrating that they leave the expedition without attempting to reach the summit at all. Climbing at altitude is hard. Even very fit people sometimes can't deal with the discomfort and pain involved and so don't make it to the summit, whereas others who are less fit succeed through sheer determination. Strong willpower and a real determination not to give up can be much more important than fitness.

DATA BOX ▸ TRAINING PLAN

A person decides on a running training programme for one month, running over hills or on a treadmill carrying a rucksack. The distances run each day are shown on the calendar.

JULY

Monday	Tuesday	Wednesday	Thursday	Friday	Saturday	Sunday
		1 8 miles	2 8 miles	3 8 miles	4 8 miles	~~5~~ DAY OFF
6 8 miles	7 8 miles	8 8 miles	9 8 miles	~~10~~ DAY OFF	11 8 miles	12 8 miles
13 8 miles	14 8 miles	~~15~~ DAY OFF	16 8 miles	17 8 miles	18 8 miles	19 8 miles
~~20~~ DAY OFF	21 8 miles	22 8 miles	23 8 miles	24 8 miles	~~25~~ DAY OFF	26 8 miles
27 8 miles	28 8 miles	29 8 miles	~~30~~ DAY OFF	31 8 miles		

CHALLENGE QUESTIONS

In the DATA BOX on this page you will see information about a running schedule or plan.

1) If a person followed this plan for the whole of July:
   a) how many times would they run on a Friday?
   b) how many times would they run on a Saturday?
   c) on which day of the week would they not get a day off?

2) If it takes about 7 minutes to run each mile, about how long will a person spend running in July if they followed this plan? Give your answer in hours and minutes.

3) A person began a training programme on 1 July. How many miles would be run in July if the pattern was:
   a) run 8 miles a day for 3 days, followed by 2 days off?
   b) run 8 miles a day for 2 days, followed by 1 day off?
   c) run 8 miles every other day?

(You will find a TIP to help you with these questions on page 28)

Climbing other high mountains will help you decide if you are ready to tackle Everest.

I f you're going to climb Everest, you should know about its history. It is a mountain that has fascinated people for a long time. For many centuries in history, mountains were frightening places where gods and monsters were thought to live and where no humans ever ventured. In more recent times, however, people have come to love mountains and to enjoy reaching their **summits**. Everest, being the highest of all the mountains in the world, is very special and now several thousand climbers from all over the world try to reach the summit each year. Most attempts are made in April or May, when the weather is least harsh.

Mount Everest

EVEREST FILE

In the DATA BOX on page 11 you will find a time line showing information about the history of Mount Everest. Use this data to help you answer these questions.

1) In which year was the mountain named Everest?

2) How many years after Everest was named:
   a) was the first expedition to the north side?
   b) was the first expedition to the south side?
   c) was the summit first reached?

3) How many years after Hillary and Tensing reached the summit in 1953:
   a) did the first woman reach the summit?
   b) was the first ascent without **oxygen**?
   c) was the first solo ascent?

(You will find a TIP to help you with these questions on page 28)

MALLORY AND IRVINE

Mallory and Irvine were two climbers who set out for the summit of Everest on 8 June 1924. They wanted to be the first to reach the summit of Everest. They were last seen in the distance by Odell, the expedition leader, but they never returned. Mallory's body was found frozen in the ice over 70 years later. It is unknown whether they ever reached the summit.

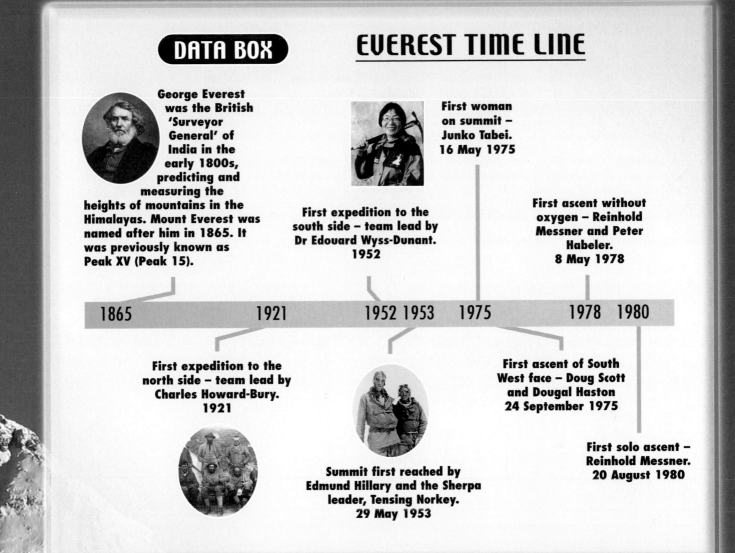

DATA BOX

EVEREST TIME LINE

George Everest was the British 'Surveyor General' of India in the early 1800s, predicting and measuring the heights of mountains in the Himalayas. Mount Everest was named after him in 1865. It was previously known as Peak XV (Peak 15).

First woman on summit – Junko Tabei. 16 May 1975

First expedition to the south side – team lead by Dr Edouard Wyss-Dunant. 1952

First ascent without oxygen – Reinhold Messner and Peter Habeler. 8 May 1978

1865   **1921**   **1952 1953**   **1975**   **1978 1980**

First expedition to the north side – team lead by Charles Howard-Bury. 1921

First ascent of South West face – Doug Scott and Dougal Haston 24 September 1975

Summit first reached by Edmund Hillary and the Sherpa leader, Tensing Norkey. 29 May 1953

First solo ascent – Reinhold Messner. 20 August 1980

BALLOON FACT

Is it possible to sail over Mount Everest in a hot air balloon? In October 1991, two balloons managed it. Both expeditions nearly ended in disaster – the first when they ran out of gas to slow their descent, and the second when the balloon's burners didn't work properly.

CHALLENGE QUESTION

1) Junko Tabei reached the summit on 16 May 1975. Doug Scott and Dougal Haston climbed the South West face on 24 September 1975. How many days are there between these dates? (Do not count the 16 May or the 24 September in your answer

2) Approximately how many hours was this?

(You will find a TIP to help you with this question on page 28)

YOUR EQUIPMENT

You need to start making preparations for your journey and choosing which items you will take with you. Make sure you take the best quality things you can – you must be sure you can rely on your equipment. How much does all of your equipment weigh? Your rucksack might not feel very heavy at home, but it will be a different story during your climb! If you have been doing weight-training, you'll find it easier to carry everything. Luckily, **yaks** will take most of the heavy equipment up the mountain, including all of the tents. Your expedition will need sleeping tents, a cook tent, a dining tent, a store tent and a toilet tent.

EVEREST FILE

In the DATA BOX on page 13 you will see the climbing equipment that you will need to take with you. The weight of each item in the list is given in grams (g).

How heavy in total are:
a) the 4 **karabiners**?
b) the 2 tape slings?
c) the sunglasses and goggles?
d) the **ascender** and **descender**?
e) the two packs?
f) the pocket knife and ice axe?
g) the harness and head lamp and bulbs?
h) the pair of **crampons** and the day pack?

CHALLENGE QUESTION

Look at the DATA BOX on page 13. What is the total weight of all the items in the list?
a) Give your answer in grams.
b) Now give your answer in kilograms.

(You will find a TIP to help you with this question on page 28)

EQUIPMENT FACTS

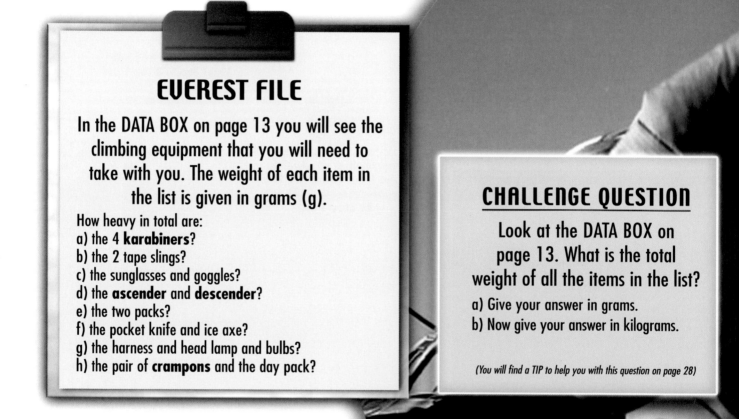

- Karabiners are metal clips which are used to join pieces of equipment to the safety harness tied around the climber. The karabiner is then clipped around the safety rope to stop the person from falling.
- A descender is normally in the shape of the number 8. It is used to create friction on the rope because it stops the rope from passing through freely. This helps to slow it down so the climber can control his or her speed when sliding down the rope.

- An ascender slides up a rope then clips in place so it can't slide back down. This is a great help for mountaineers trying to climb up the rope.
- Tape slings are loops of tape, about 50 cm long, that are used to join the various pieces of equipment (ascender, karabiner etc.) to a harness.
- Prussic loops are similar to tape slings, but are made of rope that is 6 mm thick. They can be used to make an ascender in case the climber breaks or loses the proper metal ascender.

The expedition leader will supply masks and oxygen tanks to the climbers when needed.

DATA BOX
EQUIPMENT LIST

CLIMBING EQUIPMENT		Weight
Harness	1	410g
Karabiners	4	75g each
Descender	1	280g
Ascender	1	280g
Tape Slings	2	15g each
Prussic Loops	1	10g
Ice Axe	1	500g
Crampon	2	420g
Head Lamp & Bulbs	1	180g
Pocket Knife	1	120g
Sunglasses	1	50g
Goggles	1	50g
Large Pack	1	850g
Day Pack	1	575g

OTHER EQUIPMENT

Your expedition will also need the following equipment:

Group equipment

Cooking stoves, cooking tables, eating tables and chairs, cooking equipment, eating utensils, first aid equipment, radios, satellite phone, computer, solar panels, oxygen mask, regulator and cylinders.

Personal equipment

Camera or video with plenty of film and spare batteries, repair kit, reading material, personal first aid kit, diary and writing material, sun cream, lip cream, two water bottles, personal toilet equipment, four headlamp batteries, two sleeping bags, foam mat.

Clothing

Five shirts, three jackets, two pairs of pants, two pairs of long johns, three pairs of trousers, one pair of shorts, five pairs of gloves, sun hat, warm hat, ten pairs of socks, plastic climbing boots, over boots, trekking boots, pair of **gaiters**.

THE JOURNEY TO BASE CAMP

Everyone in the expedition group flies to Kathmandu, the capital of Nepal. There are 9 men and 3 women in your group. Kathmandu is quite a distance from where you will start climbing Everest. After several days, the group flies to a town called Lhasa before driving on to **Base Camp** (BC). Base Camp is the place from where you will start the main part of your climb. Here you will stay for one week sorting your equipment and **acclimatising** to the high altitude. At all points on your journey from Kathmandu to Everest you must be very careful. The higher you travel the more likely you are to feel the effects of altitude sickness.

The Everest Base Camp.
***Sherpas** level the ground before the tents can be pitched.*

EVEREST FILE

In the DATA BOX on page 15 you will see a graph showing the percentage of **oxygen** available at different altitudes. Use the graph to answer these questions.

1) At how many metres above sea level is the percentage of oxygen:
   - a) 60%?
   - b) 50%
   - c) 80%
   - d) 67%
   - e) 35%
   - f) 91%

2) Estimate the percentage of oxygen at:
   - a) 4000 metres above sea level?
   - b) 2500 metres?
   - c) 1000 metres?
   - d) 6000 metres?
   - e) 7250 metres?
   - f) 3750 metres?

(You will find a TIP to help you with these questions on page 28)

ACCLIMATISATION FACTS

Climbing quickly to high altitudes often results in acute mountain sickness (AMS). Symptoms include some or all of the following: headache, tiredness, feeling sick, vomiting, loss of appetite, dizziness and disturbed sleep. Anyone going to high altitude can suffer from AMS.

To try to prevent AMS, climbers try to increase their altitude slowly. This is called **acclimatisation**, and it allows the body to get used to less oxygen. Acclimatisation is a slow process, taking several days.

People react to altitude differently, but most will start feeling mild symptoms of AMS in Lhasa at 3,680 m.

Altitude is how high above sea level you are. As you climb you reach higher altitudes. The higher the altitude, the more likely a person is to feel ill or get **acute mountain sickness** (AMS). This is because there is less oxygen in each breath you take as you climb higher and higher up from sea level.

This graph shows the percentage of oxygen available at different heights above sea level

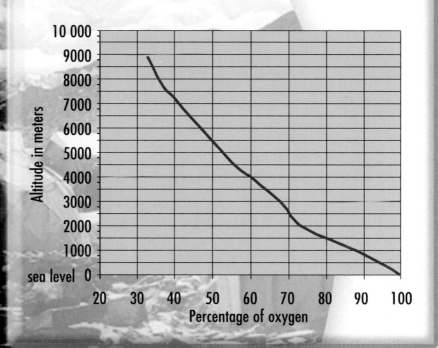

CHALLENGE QUESTION

Use the information in the DATA BOX on page 15 to help you answer these questions.

1) Approximately what percent of oxygen is gained when descending from 4000 m to 2500 m?
2) Approximately what percent of oxygen is lost when ascending from 5500 m to 8000 m?
3) Estimate how many metres are climbed as the percent of oxygen drops from 70% to 50%.

(You will find a TIP to help you with this question on page 28)

CLIMBING TO ADVANCED BASE CAMP (ABC)

You have stayed at **Base Camp** for a week, **acclimatising** to the high **altitude**. The next step is to start climbing to a point which is known as the **Advanced Base Camp (ABC)**. It is an 18 km trip and you will travel from 5,200 metres up to 6,400 metres above sea level. It will take you two days to reach ABC, so you will need to set up another camp half way up. While you are waiting at Base Camp you hire **yaks** to carry all the equipment that is needed for the rest of the climb. You need to make sure there are enough yaks to carry it. You will also need to hire experienced yak handlers to look after the animals.

EVEREST FILE

In the DATA BOX you will see some information about the yaks needed to carry your equipment to ABC. Use the information to help you answer these questions.

1) How many yak handlers would be needed to look after:
   a) 15 yaks?
   b) 24 yaks?
   c) 27 yaks?
   d) 33 yaks?

2) How many yaks would be needed to carry:
   a) 80kg?
   b) 400kg?
   c) 1000kg?
   d) 12 000kg

3) How much does it cost to hire 3 yaks and 1 yak handler for 7 days?

(You will find a TIP to help you with these questions on page 28)

The yak's long hair keeps it warm at high altitudes.

YAK FACTS

Yaks have tunnel vision, so they tend to smell their way along the trail. They also put both back hooves in exactly the same place as the front hooves, which make them very sure-footed on difficult ground.

Yaks and equipment at the Advanced Base Camp

DATA BOX KNOW YOUR YAKS

Yaks carry the heavy equipment up Everest to make it easier for the climbers.

- The yaks can only carry 20 kg on each side of their backs, so each yak carries a total of 40 kg per trip.
- For every 3 yaks there is a yak handler to look after the animals.
- Each yak costs £6.20 per day, and each yak handler costs £8.60 per day.

SHERPA FACTS

For each person climbing in an expedition there is normally a local **Sherpa** to help. The Sherpas are an ethnic group of people who come from the high mountain villages of Nepal.

As Sherpas are born at high altitude (3000 - 4000 m) they are naturally well acclimatised. However, it is only a small percentage of the Sherpas who actually excel at altitude, and many feel just as sick as Western people.

Sherpas normally have the day of the week that they were born on as first names: for example, Lhakpa means Wednesday and Nima means Sunday. As there are many names the same, Sherpas are usually called by their name, and then the name of the village that they come from. For example: Nima Sherpa from Thangboche.

CHALLENGE QUESTION

Your group has equipment weighing a total of 12 000 kg.

Use the information in the DATA BOX above and a calculator to help you find:
a) the number of yaks needed
b) the number of yak men needed
c) the cost to hire this number of yaks and yak men for 1 day
d) the cost to hire this number of yaks and yak men for 7 days

KEEPING A JOURNAL

You arrive at the **Advanced Base Camp** and set up your tents. The weather is not very good: it is very windy and snow is falling. You will be staying at ABC until the conditions improve before setting off on the last push of the climb. You have brought a journal with you and you make notes to say what you have been doing each day. Now that you are getting ready to make the last big push for the summit you are beginning to feel scared, particularly since it is so cold. You look through some reports you have brought about the weather conditions at different times of the year.

EVEREST FILE

It is important to know the **temperatures** at different places and understand how they change over time.
Answer these questions:

1) In Kathmandu, the temperature was 18°C and it rose by 14°C. What is the new temperature?
2) At **Base Camp**, the temperature was 7°C and it fell by 15°C. What is the new temperature?
3) At the summit, the temperature was -19°C and it fell by 14°C. What is the new temperature?
4) In Lhasa, the temperature was -6°C and it rose by 14°C. What is the new temperature?

(You will find a TIP to help you with these questions on page 29)

CHALLENGE QUESTIONS

Use the graph in the DATA BOX on page 19 to help you answer these questions.

1) The range is the **difference** between the maximum and minimum temperatures. What is the range for these places?
   a) Kathmandu in summer   b) Lhasa in winter   c) Base Camp in winter   d) The summit in summer
2) What is the difference between the lowest winter temperature in Kathmandu and the lowest winter temperature at the summit?
3) Which location has the greatest range between its summer high and its winter low?

(You will find a TIP to help you with these questions on page 29)

The guides try to ensure the camps are sheltered by the surrounding mountains.

DATA BOX

SUMMER AND WINTER TEMPERATURES

This chart shows maximum and minimum temperatures during summer and winter at four locations near and on Everest.

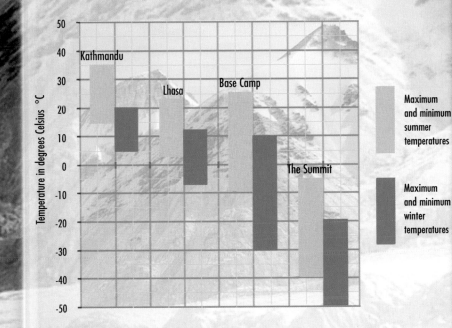

WIND FACTS

The speed of the wind affects the real temperature close to the body because it can draw away the warmer air around you. This is called 'wind chill'.

ALTITUDE FACTS

Kathmandu is 1,372 m above sea level
Lhasa is 3,680 m above sea level
Base Camp is 5,178 m above sea level
The **summit** is 8,850 m above sea level

FOOD AND DRINK

The food you take with you must be as light as possible but must provide you with lots of calories. You take biscuits and chocolate and boil-in-the-bag meals. Your body will be using between 7000 and 8000 calories a day on the mountain and so you need to keep eating as much as you can. Unfortunately though, one effect of the **altitude** is that the higher you climb, the less you feel like eating. You also need to make sure that you drink enough and do not get **dehydrated**. This can be a problem though because any water freezes and so you have to heat snow with a stove before you can have a drink.

EVEREST FILE

1) On a large 65 day expedition there are 130 people. If each person is given two eggs per day, how many eggs will be needed?
2) If about one hundredth of these eggs usually get broken on the journey, how many eggs are likely to break?
3) About how many eggs would it be sensible to take to make sure that you don't run out?

(You will find a TIP to help you with these questions on page 29)

FOOD FACTS

It is much easier to eat and drink at the main **base camps** (BC and ABC) than it is in the high camps further up, so it is important to eat well at the base camps while you can. In the higher camps you will eat boil-in-the-bag meals, or food which has been pre-cooked at the ABC and carried up to the high camps. This means that you only need to heat up this food rather than cook it properly.

At *Advanced Base Camp*, all of the water needed for cooking, drinking and washing is melted from ice.

TOILET PAPER

On Everest lots of toilet paper is needed for an expedition!

Many people use toilet paper as a handkerchief, as noses run more often when climbing. In the high camps (those above Advanced Base Camp) it is used to clean plates and cups and for mopping up any spillages. Toilet paper is also useful in the first aid kit and for cleaning out **oxygen** masks when they get clogged up inside. So in fact each person uses 1½ rolls of toilet paper every day!

COOKING FACTS

Propane is a type of gas used to cook or heat up food and to melt snow or ice to drink and wash with. Propane is also used for heating the dining tents at the main base camps (BC and ABC), so a large number of cylinders are needed for the entire expedition.

It is important not to breathe in fumes from the stoves when cooking as this can give you carbon monoxide poisoning.

CHALLENGE QUESTION

The DATA BOX above has some information about toilet paper.

Can you work out how many rolls of toilet paper are needed for the 65 day expedition of 130 people?

(You will find a TIP to help you with this question on page 29)

SETTING OFF FOR THE SUMMIT

At the **Advanced Base Camp** you must monitor the weather to pick the right moment to set off for the summit. The wind direction is important: if the wind moves just a little it can mean the difference between your climb being windy or in the shelter of the surrounding mountains. When you leave ABC you climb up a short North East facing slope to Camp 1 (C1). From there you must head North until you reach the North East ridge at about 8,500m, and then you'll climb up the rest of the North East ridge to the summit using a **fixed rope**. There are three other camps along the way – but it is hard to rest properly at such high **altitudes**.

EVEREST FILE

Make sure you know your **compass** directions when navigating and finding the wind direction.

Practise this by trying these questions:
1) If you are facing North, in which direction will you turn to face if you turn:
   a) 90° **clockwise**?
   b) 45° anticlockwise?
   c) 180°?
2) If you are facing West, in which direction will you turn to face if you turn:
   a) 90° clockwise?
   b) 45° anticlockwise?
   c) 135° clockwise?
3) If you are facing North East, in which direction will you turn to face if you turn:
   a) 90° clockwise?
   b) 270° clockwise?
   c) 45° anticlockwise?

(You will find a TIP to help you with these questions on page 29)

A fixed rope will ensure climbers don't fall and don't become lost.

 **DATA BOX**

LENGTH OF JOURNEY

As you climb Everest, journeys are usually thought of in terms of how long they take, rather than how far they are. A distance of 750 m near the summit can take 4 to 5 hours to climb whereas lower down the mountain 2000 m can be walked in 1 or 2 hours.

This table shows various stages of your journey up from Base Camp to the summit, and then the journey back to Advanced Base Camp.

Stage of journey	Starting and finishing altitudes (in metres)	Distance (in km)	Estimated time (in hours)
BC to Interim Camp	5200 – 5800	9	5 – 6
Interim Camp to ABC	5800 – 6400	9	5 – 6
ABC to Camp 1 (C1)	6400 – 7000	2	4 – 5
C1 to C2	7000 – 7500	1.25	5 – 6
C2 to C3	7500 – 7900	0.5	3 – 4
C3 to C4	7900 – 8300	0.75	4 – 5
C4 to Summit	8300 – 8850	1.25	6 – 7
Summit to C4	8850 – 8300	1.25	2 – 3
C4 to C3	8300 – 7900	0.75	1 – 2
C3 to C2	7900 – 7500	0.5	1 – 2
C2 to C1	7500 – 7000	1.25	2 – 3
C1 to ABC	7000 – 6400	2	1 – 2

SUNBURN FACTS

The sky is much clearer and free from pollution at the top of Everest and so there are much higher levels of Ultraviolet (UV) light than at sea level. UV light causes sunburn. Also, as the UV reflects off the snow, the climbers must take care to protect the face, including under the chin and nose. As the rest of our body is covered in protective clothing it is usually only necessary to use sun cream on the face and neck.

CHALLENGE QUESTIONS

The DATA BOX on page 23 shows the stages of the journey to the summit and back.

1) For each of the 7 ascent stages, convert the distance from kilometres to metres.
2) Estimate the average speed for the following journeys. Give your answer in metres per hour. Use the shortest estimated time given in the table.
a) ABC to Camp 1 (C1)
b) C1 to C2
c) C4 to C3
d) C1 to ABC

(You will find a TIP to help you with this question on page 29)

HEART RATE AND BREATHING

The climb is really difficult and you can hear your heart pumping really fast. There is less **oxygen** in the air at this height and your body is struggling to get enough. Your heart pumps faster and it makes you feel sick. Some people even hallucinate – they imagine that they see things that aren't there! This is because the lack of oxygen is playing tricks with their minds. Your breathing is heavy and you're not sure you are going to be able to make it to the **summit**. At Camp 3 (7,900 m) you will start to breathe oxygen from a tank (cylinder) which will help you to sleep before the final stages of your climb.

EVEREST FILE

The DATA BOX on page 25 shows how much oxygen a climber uses each hour.

Use the information to answer these questions:
1) When sleeping, how many litres of oxygen is used in
   - a) one minute?
   - b) ten minutes?
   - c) half an hour?
   - d) one hour?
   - e) eight hours?
   - f) 30 seconds?
   - g) 15 seconds?

2) When climbing, how many litres of oxygen is used in
   - a) one minute?
   - b) ten minutes?
   - c) half an hour?
   - d) one hour?
   - e) eight hours?
   - f) 30 seconds?
   - g) 15 seconds?

*Climbers must be aware of the potential effects of **altitude**, both on themselves and others.*

HEART AND BREATHING FACTS

The normal heart rate of an adult is between 50 and 90 beats per minute. This is called the 'resting heart rate' and is measured when a person is not doing any exercise and is not at high altitude. When you begin to exercise, the muscles in your body need more oxygen so your heart starts pumping more quickly and your breathing rate quickens. When you are at altitude there is less oxygen in the air so your heart rate and breathing need to increase even more.

If a person's oxygen tank runs out of oxygen then the body will immediately get much colder and there is a large risk of getting **frostbite**. The body would also become even more slow moving which might lead to having to spend a night out in the open. This could result in **hypothermia** and even death.

Most climbers use oxygen once they reach Camp 3.

OXYGEN TANKS

Oxygen tanks are very expensive ($400 per cylinder) so care is taken with how much is used. They can be adjusted to provide different flows of oxygen.

When sleeping, an oxygen tank is used at a flow rate of 1 litre per minute. When climbing, it is used at a flow rate of 2 litres per minute. A cylinder will last approximately 8 hours at a flow rate of 2 litre per minute.

Each person will use about 5 oxygen cylinders on the journey from Camp 3 to the summit and back as shown in this diagram.

Use of oxygen cylinders

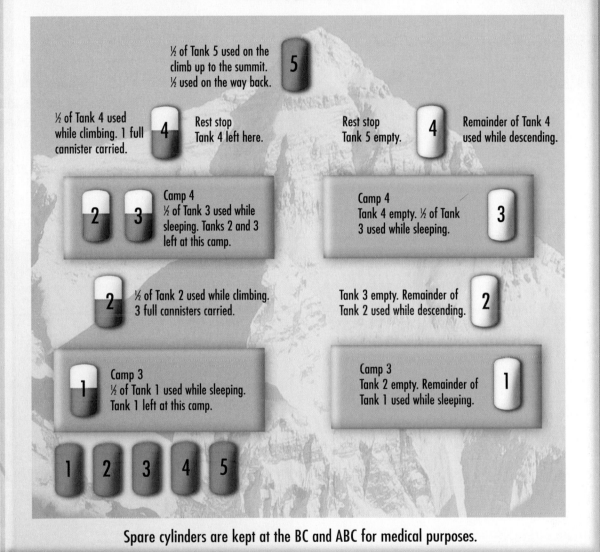

½ of Tank 5 used on the climb up to the summit. ½ used on the way back.

½ of Tank 4 used while climbing. 1 full cannister carried.

Rest stop Tank 4 left here.

Rest stop Tank 5 empty.

Remainder of Tank 4 used while descending.

Camp 4 ½ of Tank 3 used while sleeping. Tanks 2 and 3 left at this camp.

Camp 4 Tank 4 empty. ½ of Tank 3 used while sleeping.

½ of Tank 2 used while climbing. 3 full cannisters carried.

Tank 3 empty. Remainder of Tank 2 used while descending.

Camp 3 ½ of Tank 1 used while sleeping. Tank 1 left at this camp.

Camp 3 Tank 2 empty. Remainder of Tank 1 used while sleeping.

Spare cylinders are kept at the BC and ABC for medical purposes.

CHALLENGE QUESTION

An oxygen tank was used at the rate of 4 litres per minute for 1 hour, 2 litres per minute for 2 hours and 1 litre per minute for 8 hours, until it was empty. If the same oxygen tank was used at a rate of 5 litres per minute, how many hours of oxygen would it give?

(You will find a TIP to help you with this question on page 29)

REACHING THE SUMMIT

Congratulations! You've finally made it! You've managed to reach the **summit** of Mount Everest – the highest point on Earth. As you look around you, you think of all the other men and women who achieved this goal. You remember Edmund Hillary and Tenzing Norgay who first reached this point at 11:30 a.m. on 29th May, 1953. They placed three flags at the summit of Mount Everest: the flags of Britain and Nepal, and the flag of the United Nations. In the early days, most teams going to the summit were representing their countries and were very proud to plant their nation's flag on the summit.

Planting a flag at the summit is a way for the climber to mark the support of his or her team.

EVEREST FILE

The DATA BOX on this page shows some flags from different countries around the world.

Answer these questions about the flags:
1) What **fraction** of the area of:
   a) the flag of Belgium is black?
   b) the flag of Argentina is blue?
   c) the flag of Libya is green?
   d) the flag is Taiwan red?

2) Now give each of your answers to Question 1 as a percentage.

3) Which two flags have exactly the same proportion of red as each other?

4) What is the name of the shape of the Nepal flag?

(You will find a TIP to help you with these questions on page 29)

DATA BOX
YOUR EXPEDITION'S FLAGS

Argentina · Belgium · Nepal · Czech Republic

China · Greece · Libya · Austria

Taiwan · Sudan · Peru · South Africa

Russell Brice

"Climbing Mount Everest is very claustrophobic. You wear lots of clothing, big boots, big gloves, an **oxygen** mask and goggles. The goggles make it hard to see because they fog up each time that you breathe. You also wear a headlamp on your head as much of the climbing is in the dark. The climb is frustrating, because you know that you are fit and strong, but because of the **altitude** you can only take a few steps at a time. So your feeling on reaching the summit is really just relief that the climbing has finished and you can turn around and go home. Of course there is a moment of excitement, but it is not until you return to Advanced Base Camp that you are able to relax a little and then fully understand and enjoy having conquered Everest. One thing is for sure, those who have been to the top of the world have an inner confidence that will last them for the rest of their lives."

CHALLENGE QUESTION

1) About what fraction of the area of:
   a) the flag of Czech Republic is blue?
   b) the flag of Greece is blue?
   c) the flag of Sudan is green?
   d) the flag of South Africa is red?
2) Give each of your answers to Q1 as approximate percentages

(You will find a TIP to help you with this question on page 29)

TIPS FOR MATHS SUCCESS

PAGES 6–7

Subtracting large numbers:

When subtracting numbers with lots of digits, make sure that you line all the digits up so that the units line up with the units, tens with the tens, hundreds with the hundreds and so on.

CHALLENGE QUESTIONS

One way of working out how to multiply a number by 8 is to double the number, then double your answer and then double the answer again.

For example, 125 x 8 =

125 doubled = 250   250 doubled = 500

500 doubled = 1000   so 125 x 8 = 1000

Another way of converting miles into kilometres is to multiply the number by 1.6

PAGES 8–9

When reading a calendar, look at the column headings that show the days of the week. Each of the dates in one column will be the same day of the week.

PAGES 10–11

Finding the difference between years:

To find how many years there are between two dates, subtract one from the other. Make sure that you line all the digits up so that the units line up with the units, tens with the tens, hundreds with the hundreds and so on.

```
   1936
 – 1865
 _____
     71
```

so 1936 is 71 years after 1865.

CHALLENGE QUESTION

First find how many days there are from 17th May to 31st May. Add to your answer the number of days in June (30), July (31), August (31), and the number of days in September up to the 23rd (23).

PAGES 12–13

Kilograms and grams

Remember that there are 1000 grams in 1 kilogram. To change a measurement in grams to kilograms, divide the number of grams by 1000, e.g. 4370 g = 4.37 kg.

PAGES 14–15

Reading graphs

- To find the altitude for a given oxygen percentage: go straight up from the percentage until you reach the line and then go across.
- To find the oxygen percentage for a given altitude: go straight across from the altitude until you reach the line and then go down.

PAGES 16–17

When dividing numbers by 3 it might help you to know the numbers in the 3 times table

1 x 3 = 3	5 x 3 = 15	9 x 3 = 27
2 x 3 = 6	6 x 3 = 18	10 x 3 = 30
3 x 3 = 9	7 x 3 = 21	
4 x 3 = 12	8 x 3 = 24	

When dividing by 40, first divide by 10 and then divide by 4.

PAGES 18–19

Negative numbers:

When finding temperature rises, move to the right on the number line. When finding temperature falls, move to the left on the number line.

```
-10 -9 -8 -7 -6 -5 -4 -3 -2 -1 0 1 2 3 4 5 6 7 8 9 10
```

28

ANSWERS ANSWERS ANSWERS

PAGES 16–17

EVEREST WORK

1) a) 5
   b) 8
   c) 9
   d) 11

2) a) 2
   b) 10
   c) 25
   d) 300

3) £190.40

CHALLENGE QUESTION

a) 300
b) 100
c) £2720
d) £19,040

PAGES 18–19

EVEREST WORK

1) 32°C
2) –8°C
3) –33°C
4) 8°C

CHALLENGE QUESTION

1) a) 20°C
   b) 19°C
   c) 40°C
   d) 35°C

2) 55°C

3) Base Camp

PAGES 20–21

EVEREST WORK

1) 16 900
2) 169
3) about 17 070

CHALLENGE QUESTION

12,675 toilet rolls

PAGES 22–23

EVEREST WORK

1) a) E
   b) NW
   c) S

2) a) N
   b) SW
   c) NE

3) a) SE
   b) NW
   c) N

CHALLENGE QUESTIONS

1) 9000 m 9000 m 2000 m 1250 m
   500 m 750 m 1250 m

2) a) 500 m per hour
   b) 250 m per hour
   c) 750 m per hour
   d) 2000 m per hour

PAGES 24–25

EVEREST WORK

1) a) 1 litre
   b) 10 litres
   c) 30 litres
   d) 60 litres
   e) 480 litres
   f) ½ litre or 500 ml
   g) ¼ litre or 250 ml

2) a) 2 litres
   b) 20 litres
   c) 60 litres
   d) 120 litres
   e) 960 litres
   f) 1 litre
   g) ½ litre or 500 ml

CHALLENGE QUESTION

3.2 hours, or 3 hours 12 minutes

PAGES 26–27

EVEREST WORK

1) a) $\frac{1}{3}$
   b) $\frac{2}{3}$
   c) $\frac{1}{1}$ or 1
   d) $\frac{3}{4}$

2) a) 33%
   b) 66%
   c) 100%
   d) 75%

3) Austria and Peru
4) pentagon

CHALLENGE QUESTION

1) a) $\frac{2}{8}$ or $\frac{1}{4}$
   b) Just over $\frac{5}{9}$
   c) $\frac{2}{12}$ or $\frac{1}{6}$
   d) $\frac{5}{24}$

2) a) 25%
   b) about 55%
   c) about 16% or 17%
   d) about 21%

GLOSSARY

ADVANCED BASE CAMP (ABC) A rest camp on Everest at 6400 m.

ACCLIMATISATION The way your body gets used to less oxygen at higher altitude.

ACUTE MOUNTAIN SICKNESS (AMS) The sickness that is experienced at high altitudes.

ALTITUDE Height above sea level.

ASCENDER A piece of equipment which helps you to climb up a rope by stopping you from slipping down.

BASE CAMP (BC) A rest camp on Everest at 5200 m.

CARDIOVASCULAR To do with the heart.

COMPASS A tool for finding north, and therefore helping you navigate. It usually shows the eight compass points N, NE, E, SE, S, SW, W and NW.

CRAMPON A framework with spikes on the bottom. It fits over a boot to provide better grip on icy ground.

DEHYDRATE When you do not drink enough water.

DESCENDER A piece of equipment which helps you to control your speed when sliding down a rope.

FIXED ROPE A rope that is left in one position to help all members of an expedition up a climb.

FROSTBITE Damage caused to the skin when it is exposed to extremely cold weather for a long period of time (usually the toes, fingers, or face are affected). In severe cases, the harm is permanent.

GAITERS Waterproof coverings for the lower leg.

HYPOTHERMIA Where the body temperature drops and a person becomes very cold.

INTERIM CAMP A rest camp on Everest at 5800 m, halfway between Base Camp and Advanced Base Camp.

KARABINER A metal clip used to join pieces of equipment.

NAVIGATION Finding your way.

OXYGEN A gas that all animals need to breathe.

SHERPA An ethnic group of Tibetan people, used as expert guides on many Himalayan mountaineering expeditions.

SUMMIT The highest point.

YAK Large long-haired wild ox of Tibet, used for carrying equipment.

MATHS GLOSSARY

ANGLE A measure of turn.

DEGREES The units used for measuring angle °, or temperature °C.

CLOCKWISE To make a turn in the direction that the hands of a clock move. Anti-clockwise is to turn in the opposite direction.

DIFFERENCE The difference between two numbers can be found by subtracting (taking away) the smaller number from the larger number.

ESTIMATE To find a number or amount that is close to an exact number.

FRACTIONS These are made when shapes or numbers are split into equal parts. For example, if a shape is cut into 6 equals parts each part is one sixth or $\frac{1}{6}$.

NEGATIVE NUMBERS Numbers on the other side of zero from positive numbers, such as - 4, -2, -12 etc. Temperatures below 0°C are negative numbers and show freezing conditions.

PERCENTAGE A part out of 100.

TEMPERATURE How hot or cold something is. It is usually measured in degrees Celsius which are written using the symbols °C.

PICTURE CREDITS
Front cover: Bill Crouse
Bill Crouse: 4-5, 6-7, 8-9, 12-13, 14-15, 20-21, 22-23, 24-25, 26-27, 29 (centre).
Russell Brice: 17 (inset), 18-19, 24 (inset), 29 (far left, left, right, far right), 30.
Shutterstock: 10-11 Wang Sanjun, 16-17 Jason Maehl.
Robert Bosch: 27 (inset).

Every effort has been made to trace the copyright holders, and we apologize in advance for any unintentional omissions.
We would be pleased to insert the appropriate acknowledgements in any subsequent edition of this publication.